7 *EASY* Steps to Goal Setting Success

I0161555

PAM PALAGYI

Arise
PUBLISHING

7 Easy Steps to Goal Setting Success

Pam Palagyi

Copyright © Pam Palagyi 2015

ISBN 978-0-9964062-4-6

All rights reserved.

Published by ARISE PUBLISHING

No part of this publication shall be reproduced, transmitted, or sold in whole or part in any form without prior written consent of the author. All logos and graphics are property of Arise Ministries.

This guide is not intended to be a source of legal, business, accounting, or financial advice. It is based on the author's opinions, experiences, and leadership training. The reader assumes all responsibilities for the use of this information.

Introduction

Goal setting is a journey. It is a lifetime excursion of personal challenge and adventure. Imagine what your life could look like 12 months from now!

7 Easy Steps to Goal Setting Success is a powerful tool to help you along the way. The process establishes a balanced approach to living for all areas of your life. It will help you to build a strategic roadmap for the future and identify your deepest desires.

By the end of the book, after you have completed all *7 Steps*, you will have in your hands...

- **A life outline with all of your hopes, dreams, and desires.**

- **An understanding of the 6 Life Systems and how they fit into your plans.**

- **A yearly overview of your goals for the next 365 days.**

- **A 90 Day Action Plan to motivate and energize you to achieve your goals.**

- **A balanced and healthy approach to personal growth.**

Every plan requires time to process and implement. Set some time aside to go through each of the *7 Steps*. This guide is not a quick fix, but a comprehensive approach to growth and development. It is balanced and will encourage healthy habits in all areas of your life. Invest the time in yourself!

If you are an experienced goal-setter, *7 Steps* provides easy to use forms to jump start you into the next year. If you are a novice to goal setting, the guide will get you started on the right path.

Wherever you are now, there is a way forward and a plan for your life. The Prophet Jeremiah wrote these words thousands of years ago:

> *"For I know the plans I have for you," declares the LORD, "plans to prosper you and not to harm you, plans to give you hope and a future." Jeremiah 29:11*

When we can tap into God's plan for our life, all things become possible.

Blessings!

Table of Contents

Chapter One

WHY SET GOALS?

An archer cannot hit the bull's-eye if he doesn't know where the target is. Anonymous

C an setting goals change your life?

Just ask these people...

Jennifer earned her Ph.D. and now teaches at a university.

John and Joanne enjoyed two weeks of sun and fun in Hawaii.

Patrick wrote and published his first book.

Joyce graduated from college at the age of 74.

Anna lost 57 pounds in just three months.

What makes each of these people and events remarkable?

They all set goals and then worked hard to achieve them!

Whether it is losing those extra pounds, saving for that once-in-a-lifetime vacation, or reaching for your dreams, there is a way for the impossible things to become possible. And the best way to do that is by setting goals. Once you get focused and develop an action plan, positive results will follow!

The 7 *Step* approach uncovers those hidden and forgotten ideas and makes them a reality. It ensures a healthy, balanced approach to living. With the 7 *Step* approach you can and will grow in every area of your life...even those problematic ones.

As we begin the goal setting journey together, we will start with the fundamentals. What are goals? Why are they important?

What is a Goal?

Goals help us to make meaningful progress towards our dreams. They launch us into the realms of possibility.

A goal is an aim, ambition, or objective which is achievable through planned and directed effort.

Goals are our path forward. They provide us with a destination, a life map.

If we were planning a vacation, we would start the trip knowing our journey's end. We chart a course and off we go.

There may be different routes, some more direct and others more scenic. We may run into traffic jams, roadblocks, and construction delays. If we are determined, we press through the obstacles because of the benefits once we arrive.

I have never stopped my car, turned around and said "This isn't worth it. I'll just cancel vacation this year!"

Goals function in the very same way. They give us an endpoint, a destination to work towards. Like the roadmap, they guide our decisions and actions and give us a course to follow.

What would you like to achieve in your lifetime?

What is your passion?

What problem unsettles you and demands attention?

How do you plan on seeing your ideas come to pass?

Once you choose the targets, then you can implement your specific actions and follow up to achieve those goals. That's what *7 Easy Steps to Goal Setting Success* is all about.

This is not a micro-managing approach to life. We will not schedule every minute or jam the day with activity. It is not a magic formula. Nor is it a complex series of actions that keep you busy, but not productive.

7 Steps is designed to be a lifestyle change, not a one-time exercise. This book provides a balanced and healthy approach to living where you are in control.

You set the goals.

You do the work.

You enjoy the benefits!

> Setting goals is the first step in turning the invisible into the visible.
>
> **Tony Robbins**

Chapter Two

THE BENEFITS Of GOALS

Goals that are not written down are just wishes.
Anonymous

S etting goals and successfully completing them are the foundation for a disciplined, productive life. I am a natural goal setter. When I see an endpoint, I then figure out the steps to get me there and begin to move forward. But not everyone is wired like that. Before we get started, let me encourage you with ten reasons why you should consider setting goals:

#1 Goals define who we are. We are all different. We have varied gifts, experiences, hopes, and dreams. Because of this, no two people will have identical destinations. Each will find their own individual path. When we set our targets, they are an expression of who we are and where we want to go. Goals are an extension of who we are.

#2 Goals propel us forward. They are designed to motivate us to take action. Instead of worrying about our present condition, goals provide the inspiration to move us forward towards a desired endpoint.

#3 Goals organize our desires, time, and priorities. When we set goals, we put ourselves in the driver's seat. What is important? How do we make time for it? We become the one who controls our decisions. We elevate

our priorities to the top of the list when we take charge.

#4 Goals stretch us. They become a catalyst for growth. We use those dormant muscles which have atrophied over time…ouch! That hurts! But the saying "no pain, no gain" holds true even here. Goals compel us to get out of our comfort zone and begin to move.

#5 Goals boost our confidence. Once we get past the initial stage of inertia, our confidence grows. When I began going to the gym to get in shape, I was excited and confidant even after the first week. I was in motion, taking control, and it revved my engine. I began to visualize how I would look and feel when I achieved my goal. My self-confidence grew and I was motivated to see it through.

#6 Goals give clarity of vision. When we have a target in mind, whether it is long range or short range, our vision is clear and our path direct. What would you like to achieve over a lifetime? Where would you like to live? What is your once-in-a-lifetime vacation?

#7 *Goals provide perspective.* They serve as signposts in our life journey. Like a highway marker, goals tell us where we are, how far we have come, and how much further we have to go.

#8 *Goals establish a standard.* A high jumper doesn't enter the field wondering how high the bar might be. He knows exactly where it will be positioned. And he also realizes the bar will be raised and reset continually before the winner will be determined. Goals function in the same way. They provide us with a preset standard, a personal heigth to reach towards.

#9 *Goals keep us focused.* They become the roadmap to our future. Like any highway, the easiest and quickest route is to stay on the main road and avoid the side trips. When you have a chosen itinerary planned, goals help to keep us on that direct path.

#10 *Goals lead to a full and meaningful life.* They help us realize our purpose and calling. Goals help us to achieve our highest potential with a sense of satisfaction.

Each of us has a divine purpose, one that matches the gifts and talents we've been given. Life is filled with a series of destinations, achievements, and opportunities to express those gifts.

Goals let us focus on those things which are most important to who we have been created to be. They assist us in fulfilling our lifelong mission. Once we set those significant targets, our life gains momentum and new meaning.

Landing on the Moon

In May of 1961, President John F. Kennedy issued a challenge. He set the goal of landing a man on the moon by the end of the decade.

Kennedy was eager for the U.S. to take the lead in the Space Race in the 1960's. Known as the Apollo project, it overcame many obstacles:

- The high cost of 40 billion dollars

- The refusal of joint cooperation from Russia

- A disastrous accident when Apollo 1 exploded

Kennedy's lofty goal was accomplished on July 20,1969. The Apollo 11 mission landed astronauts Neil Armstrong, Buzz Aldrin, and their Lunar Module on the Moon.

Are You a Goal Setter or a Problem-Solver?

OK... not everyone has a positive emotional response to setting goals! Maybe the thought of setting goals makes you tense.

Not everyone is an enthusiastic goal setter. Some of us are better suited to problem solving. When the subject of goals comes up, we clench our teeth and grimace. But why?

In his book *Stop Setting Goals If You Would Rather Solve Problems,* Bobb Biehl identifies two types of people: **goal-setters** and **problem-solvers.**

The difference? Those who like to set goals are looking for new objectives, fresh ideas, and projects. They want to create. They are fixers.

Problem-solvers are people who are more inclined to ask "How could we improve what already exists?" They don't look for new items on the agenda when the old ones still aren't working right. Neither perspective is wrong, just different vantage points.

Both problem-solvers and goal-setters can work together in planning and finding a way forward. One group plays the offense; the other the defense.

Let's assume Coach A and B oversee the high school baseball team. Coach A is a goal setter. He tells the team, "This year we are going to win the league championship and go to the regional playoffs!" His lofty goal gets set.

Coach B cringes. He knows one major obstacle standing in the way of Coach A's dream. The team must improve their fielding technique. Last season they lost 25% of their games because of careless errors.

Who's right? Is Coach B a killjoy, or does he just focus on the problem instead of the final outcome? Does the team need to improve? Absolutely. One sees the vision of the championship, the other the major obstacle preventing it from happening.

If you are someone who is a problem-solver, you can still respond positively to these *7 Steps.* Instead of "What do I need to accomplish?" ask yourself...

- **"Where do I need to improve?"**

- **"What problems need solving?"**

- **"How can I maximize what already exists?"**

Biehl defines success as "the feeling you get when you reach the goals you have set or when you have solved the problems you decided to solve."

Setting goals (or solving problems!) produces balance, discipline, and direction. The result is a satisfying, fulfilled life where you are realizing your purpose and accomplishing your dreams!

Before we actually begin to set those life-changing goals, let's look at a few basics concepts. These will help us to frame our goal-setting model in order to maximize the results.

---- Chapter Three ----

The B.E.S.T. Goals

*An average person with average talent, ambition and
education, can outstrip the most brilliant genius in
our society, if that person has clear, focused goals.*
Brian Tracy

How do we choose our goals?

How do we know if they are credible?

Goals should be defined in such a way so that they are both practical
and functional. As we record each of our targets, we want to be clear
about our objectives.

In order to do this, we need a model that has a proven track record.
It should be simple, memorable, but still help us to hone our desires
in a specific way.

One method uses the acrostic **"B.E.S.T."** When our goals are
Believable, Energizing, Specific, and **Time Bound**, we are much
more likely to see them come to pass.

We will describe each letter before we proceed further. We want our
objectives to be…

   B…Believable In other words, they should be attainable.

Our targets should be achievable within a given context. Some of them may be a stretch, but still not unrealistic or outright fantasy.

"I am going to be a *New York Times* best-selling author this year" is a fantasy when you haven't even started your book. But, determining to write the first draft to the book might be a solid possibility. Pitching to several editors or self-publishing and becoming an Amazon best-seller is feasible. Allow yourself to dream, but keep it real.

E...Energizing Goals should motivate us to complete them. A **"B.E.S.T."** goal should inspire us to take action.

Get a picture in your mind or on paper of what it would be like to hit that target. Allow the desire to awaken your creativity.

Goals are not meant to weigh us down or control our every action. Instead, they should uplift our expectations and encourage us to meet the challenge.

S...Specific Each area should be well defined. "I want to be smarter" is too broad of a statement. Zone in on that exact target.

"I want to expand my knowledge of American history" is more definitive. That leads to establishing a smaller objective. "I will read one presidential biography every month."

T...Time Bound Give yourself a time frame for completion. Have a starting and finishing date will help you to prioritize it on the yearly calendar.

Open-ended goals are far too easy to ignore. "I'll get around to it when I have the time." But, it is never the right time! When we draw the line in the sands of time and link our intentions to a fixed point, we are much more likely to start acting upon it and developing a plan.

For example, if I want to shed some pounds, my goal would not be "I want to lose weight this year." A better approach would be "I want to lose fifty pounds in six months." Then I can break that down in time segments with smaller goals, i.e. "this month I will lose 10 pounds."

When we choose our goals, they should not be impossible, but within the realm of probability. We can envision high, lofty dreams as long as they are coupled with realistic action steps. With a plan, perseverance, and faith, they are attainable!

Awake the Sleeping Giant Within!

How do we take our ideas and make them a reality? The key to activating our intelligence and creativity starts with one simple act...

WRITE THE GOALS DOWN!

What difference could that make?

Study after study shows that writing goals triggers a hidden power. Writing our intentions on paper actually enables us to take those desires and make them a reality.

It all has to do with how our brain functions.

Each of us has a part in our brain called the **Reticular Activating System.** The **RAS** is a set of nuclei in our brain stem that is responsible for regulating mental wakefulness and alertness.

When we focus on a goal by recording it, the RAS section of the brain goes into action. It begins to exert control in order to meet those expectations. The RAS becomes a power plant generating possible scenarios. It functions like a built-in motivational coach and helps to achieve those written goals!

When I wrote 7 *Steps*, I gave myself six weeks to rewrite, edit, and format the guide. Almost half of that time took place during a family vacation. How would I have the time to complete the book?

My RAS went into action and offered several scenarios. I could write in the evening, but I am usually too tired. I could write in the afternoon, but that is when I spend "adult" time with family members.

I decided to rise early each morning between 4 and 5 o'clock. This meant I had to rearrange my sleep schedule, but it was doable. My brain made the adjustments and my body followed. That is how the RAS works. It finds the way forward and makes the impossible, possible.

When we are ready to set our goals, we will refer back to the B.E.S.T. model. If our goals are Believable, Energizing, Specific, and Time Bound, they will give us a clear roadmap of how to act. Defining our targets and writing them down increases the probability of seeing them come to pass.

The Road West

On May 10, 1869, the first Transcontinental Railroad joined the eastern and the western halves of the United States.

In this monumental feat, the Union Pacific Railroad pushed eastward and the Central Pacific Railroad spread west. The companies blasted through mountains, weathered adverse conditions, and laid track for over 1756 miles.

Their goal? To unite the country after the Civil War had torn the United States apart. This epic accomplishment opened a faster, easier way of travel between the coasts.

After six years of backbreaking labor, the "Last Spike" was driven into the ground. The track was finished and travel from east to west became possible.

Chapter Four

THE SIX LIFE SYSTEMS

What you get by achieving your goals is not as important as what you become by achieving your goals. Zig Ziglar

O ur body is composed of many systems…the circulatory, skeletal, muscular, nervous, reproductive, digestive, and respiratory system. They all work together to ensure we function as a healthy, human being.

In the same way, our life consists of six distinct systems. Each of these contribute to our overall health and vibrancy. While our body systems are internal, our life systems are external. I call these the **6 Life Systems**: spiritual, financial, social, physical, mental, and professional.

Each of these areas is independent of the other and yet interdependent at the same time. For example, our physical well-being influences our mental state. And the professional system impacts the financial. They are linked together.

Each **Life System** is…

- **Distinct, but influences the others.**

- **Necessary for a balanced, healthy life.**

- **External.**

- **Subject to our control.**

- **Calling for attention.**

We may prefer to work in only one or two of the systems. Usually it is because that area is more enjoyable. Our natural personality and habits make it easier to gravitate towards that specific system. Maybe we have had success in the past. But we can't afford to ignore the other five spheres.

As we begin the process of goal setting, we are going to explore the separate **6 Life Systems** and design our goals to fit into each of these categories.

Spiritual. This area contains all of the components that nurture our spiritual being. For a Christian, that might include Bible reading, Bible study, prayer, books to read, conferences to attend, church attendance, service, and character traits to work on throughout the year. We can even define a year with a single, overarching word like "integrity," a quote, or a scripture verse. How will we grow spiritually in the next year?

Financial. This system focuses on how much money is earned, as well as how it is spent. It includes developing a budget and making contributions for lasting financial stability. Debt-free living is also something to consider. Others possibilities might be paying off a house or maybe saving enough to make the down payment on your first home. We want to look at the short-term necessity of paying those monthly bills, but also include long-term planning.

Social. These goals connect to our intimate and social relationships. In the midst of a busy schedule, our close relationships are usually the first thing to suffer. In this area we define when and how we relate to the important people in our life. A small shift in our social interactions can be life-changing, not only for us but also for our loved ones. Our spouse, children, parents, friends and extended family need quality time. That may require a change in our priorities in order to meet their needs.

Physical. We have already mentioned weight loss, but what about our overall health? Are we physically fit for our age? Do we get an annual physical? What could we do to improve our total body fitness? Exercise? Drink eight glasses of water a day? Learn a new sport? We need to accept our limitations, but also consider the possibilities. How we maintain our physical health affects the success of other areas where we have set goals.

Mental. These goals relate to our mental well-being and growth. How do we expand and nurture our mind? This includes major items like educational goals, but also smaller targets. How many books will we read or listen to per year? If we are of retirement age, our goal may be keeping our minds active and alert. How we think and what we think about directs our actions.

Professional. This last system of life includes our current job, advancement, and lifelong career. Do we have aspirations for promotion? What would that require of us? Are we content or should we consider a career change? What about starting our own business? Our professional life can grow in many ways. Experience, training, and opportunity are just a few examples. What are our plans for that growth?

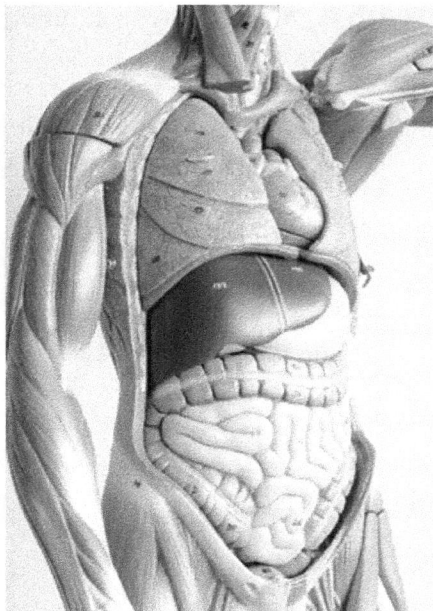

These **Six Life Systems** are an essential part of every person's life. Keeping each area vibrant and healthy is what goal-setting is all about. As we move into the *7 Steps* phase, we will be working within the context of each Life System.

We have just laid the basic foundation for setting successful goals. Now it's time to implement the *7 Easy Steps to Goal Setting Success!*

A Massive Building Project

Nehemiah was a man who sacrificed his title and position to see God's will come to pass. As a servant to King Artaxerxes, he willingly relinquished his place as cup-bearer to the king when the call to action came.

Nehemiah traveled hundreds of miles back to the war-ravaged nation of Israel.

The goal?

To lead Israel's refugees in a massive reconstruction project. The walls of Jerusalem were in shambles and its inhabitants unprotected from invaders.

Nehemiah rallied the exiles, organized the building project, and rebuilt the walls of the city.

Though Nehemiah faced constant criticism and opposition from all sides, he kept his goal before him.

Fifty-two days later the wall was complete.

Chapter Five

STEP #1: THE WRAP UP

Learn from the past, set vivid, detailed goals for the future, and live in the only moment of time over which you have any control: now. Denis Waitley

Before we start, I suggest you read through each of the *7 Steps* to get an understanding of how each one builds upon the other. You may be tempted to skip one, but complete each step before moving on to the next.

The *7 Steps* are:

1. The Wrap Up

2. Goal-storming

3. Assign a Time Frame

4. Prioritize the Goals

5. Make an Action Plan

6. Review the Goals Regularly

7. Celebrate

Here are some suggestions to make this process easier and more enjoyable:

Set aside a specific time to process each step. Find a quiet place and turn off all distractions. Reflect, think, and make decisions about the course of your life. If you don't have an entire day, carve out an hour over several days. If you are married, you may go through the *7 Steps* together.

I suggest that you make an appointment with yourself and keep it. Invest in your future...you are worth it!

Begin with prayer. If you are a spiritual person, invite God and His wisdom into the process. He knows the plans He has for you and can inspire you into new realms of possibility!

Write down everything. You can edit later. Use the *7 Step Workbook.*(see link below) The forms included in the workbook were created to simplify the process. Or you may record them in a journal or on your computer.

Review your list of goals when you are done. Let the dust settle and be sure of your direction forward.

The forms for each of the *7 Steps* are available fin the *7Steps Workbook.* Download a free copy at this web page:

http://pampalagyi.com/7-steps-workbook/

The Wrap Up

In order to set a course, we first need to understand our present location. It's like those maps in the mall...You are here! Once we pinpoint our present location, we can map out a course to get us to our destination.

The Wrap Up step accomplishes this. We can bring closure to those areas that need it and highlight our areas of strength. Reviewing our past gives us a fresh perspective on where to make improvements. It provides focus for the next segment of time as we look towards setting goals.

During this step, try to consider all of the **6 Life Systems** and evaluate each one. For convenience, we will approach the *7 Steps* as though we are wrapping up the end of a calendar year. Whenever you are ready, that is the best time to start. If you begin in March, June, or September, complete this step before going to Step #2. Just adjust the forms and questions accordingly.

As you begin, use the *Wrap Up Form* and ask yourself these questions...

What did I do right last year?

- Where was I successful?

- What did I accomplish?

- How did I do it?

Where could I have improved?

- Where are those reoccurring troublesome areas?

- Where do I struggle?

31

- Do I have any regrets?

What do I need to eliminate?

- What robs me of time and energy?

- What activities or relationships have exceeded their expiration date?

- Have I outgrown certain activities?

What do I need to add?

- What is missing from my life?

- What areas cry out for attention?

- Where do I need more time and energy?

- Where do I need to shift my priorities?

Do I need to forgive anyone?

- Where do I need to forgive myself?

- Where do I need to ask forgiveness?

Am I able to close the door to this past year and move into the future?

- What is preventing that from happening? How can I resolve the issue?

- How do I release past successes and failures?

After you complete the **Wrap Up Form**, take a deep breath. Celebrate your successes! Rejoice over all the things that you did right. Don't wallow in past failures or disappointments and allow them to dampen your readiness to move on. This is the time to release the past and begin to look to the future. With Step #2, we will begin to take control of your life.

Chapter Six

STEP #2: GOAL-STORMING

Set your goals high enough to inspire you and low enough to encourage you. Anonymous

In this second step, we are going to brainstorm every area of life. We will consider each of the **6 Life Systems** and record every dream, hope, and desire.

It's a total brain-drain of all of our ambitions both present and future. This process takes our random thoughts out of our mind and onto paper. It puts them into written, tangible form.

I call it Goal-Storming!

As we get ready for this exercise, open yourself up to the possibilities. Don't second guess your dreams or limit yourself. Record even the most outrageous vision you may have, even if it seems improbable!

Write down anything that captures your imagination in each area. If you want to be a ski instructor one day, write it down. If you hope to have a million dollars in the bank, record that aspiration. Give yourself permission to dream BIG. Be willing to take a risk.

At this stage, we are not going to assign time frames or worry about our goals fitting the **B.E.S.T.** model. We only want to record every thought and then we will edit and define specific goals in a later step.

Now, find a comfortable, quiet place where you will not be disturbed. Give yourself at least an hour to complete this step. Take your time and be thorough recording your current aspirations as well as future ones.

Use the questions from the *101 Goal-Storming Questions* page to stimulate your creative brain. Let your mind dislodge all of that hidden potential!

Record your ideas on the *Goal-Storming Form.* You may need to print multiple copies of this form. Download the free *7 Steps Workbook* at:

http://pampalagyi.com/7-steps-workbook/

Chapter Seven

STEP #3: ASSIGN A TIME FRAME

A goal is a dream with a deadline. Napoleon Hill

Every goal needs a time frame, an endpoint that limits and focuses our efforts to achieve it. In this step we will review each goal from the **Goal-Storming Form** and assign each a reasonable time frame.

Some goals are accomplished in a day.

Others take a week or a month.

Many require years or a lifetime to fulfill.

The daily targets lead to hitting the monthly goals. The monthly objectives contribute to accomplishing the yearly goals.

For example, a long term goal of writing a book would be broken into smaller goal segments. Our daily target might be to write, edit, or research for one hour every night. Our short term goal could be to finish writing one chapter a month. Both of these contribute to reaching the yearlong aim of writing a book.

Or maybe we want to lose that extra fifty pounds. We change our daily eating habits, exercise five times per week, and set a goal of reducing our weight ten pounds every month. Over the course of five months, our goal will be met!

When we set a time frame, we must be definitive. Words like *someday, one day*, or *maybe* are not defining terms. Eliminate those wishy-washy words!

When we assign a time frame to our goals, we need to pause and consider several factors that could influence the achievement of it:

- How much time and energy can I devote to it?

- What priority will this particular target have in relation to the rest of my life?

- What resources do I need to help?

- Are there any obstacles that might get in the way?

- Do I need advice from a professional?

As we consider each of our **Goal-Storming** targets, we will assign a time frame to each. We want to begin thinking in tangible blocks of time. Our targets fall into one of four classifications: daily, weekly, yearly, or lifelong.

Daily Goals

The simplest type is a daily goal. These are set and met on a regular basis. They require day-to-day attention and include such things as…

Exercise…walk thirty minutes a day.

Bible reading…read three chapters of the Bible every day.

Work-related tasks…read and answer emails by 10 am.

Short-Term Goals

These are goals are realized within weeks, months, even up to a year. They include such things as...

Read two books per month.

Save 10% of my income.

Make weekly phone calls to family members.

Long-Term Goals

Long term goals require an extended period of time, from one to five years. Most of us need more of these long range targets to capture our imagination and motivate us towards future endeavors. These might include...

Earn a college degree

Save for an Alaskan cruise

Run a marathon.

Lifetime Goals

These goals are met throughout an entire life. They define our life and direct our decisions. Sometimes these are specific and long-range like...

Write 10 books

Leave $100,000 to each of my grandchildren

Lifetime goals may seem more like standards to live by. But these are more than guiding principles if they can separated into concrete actions...

Commitment to love and honor my spouse.(This might include weekly date nights, renewing of vows on a regular basis, Marriage Enrichment seminars every two years)

Look at each of the goals written down on the *Goal-Storming Form*. Label each as *D* for daily, *S* for short-term, *L* for long-term, and *LT* for life time goals.

Write your designation under the "Time Frame" column beside each goal.

Step # 2: Goal-Storming
Step # 3: Assign a Time

Record your goals for each of the Six Life Systems: Spiritual, Physical, Mental, Social, Financial, and Vocational. Use the 101 Goal-Setting Questions sheet as a guide. Assign a time frame to each goal: LT (Lifetime), L (Long-term), S (Short-term), D (Daily).

TIME FRAME	GOAL
LT	Play golf throughout my life
L	Create a family photographic history
S	Lose 50 pounds
L	Write and publish my first book
D	Exercise daily
S	Save 6 months worth of income
L	Pay off my mortgage
S	Read through the Bible this year
L	Vacation in Hawaii
L	Get promoted to Program Director position
L	Learn how to speak Spanish
S	Read 24 books this year
S	Spend 1 weekend on a spiritual retreat
S/D	Invest iquality time into family relationships
LT	Travel to all the continents of the world
L	Teach my daughters and granddaughters to sew
S/D	Get rid of clutter in my home

www.pamgaslayi.com

Chapter Eight

STEP #4: PRIORITIZE THE GOALS

Discipline is the bridge between goals and accomplishment. Jim Rohn

At this point, we have recorded our goals and assigned a reasonable time frame to each. Obviously, it would be impossible to work on them all at once. Now we decide which will receive our immediate attention. We are going to prioritize.

First we separate our master **Goal-Storming Form** into the six different categories of goals according to the **6 Life Systems.** Then, we will choose which ones to attack first.

Because most people plan on a yearly basis, we will approach the rest of our planning with that in mind. However, adapt the forms and process to whatever works best for you.

6 Life Systems Forms

The first part is to transfer each of the goals from the **Goal-Storming Form** onto one of the **6 Life Systems Pages**. You will find separate pages for each category...Mental, Physical, Social, Spiritual, Financial, and Professional. Each form has sections for lifetime, long-term, short-term, and daily goals. As you go through the list, ask yourself which is the best category for the goal.

Transfer all of the goals from your *Goal-Storming Form* to each *Life System Page* according to their category.

Example using Physical goals:

Lifetime...maintain a healthy body

Long-term...run a marathon

Short-term...jog five times a week

Daily...drink 8 glasses of water a day

Write these on the *Physical Life System Page.*

Write down each separate goal according to its time frame on the matching *Life System Page.* Is it a Lifetime, Long-term, Short-term, or Daily goal?

Use the B.E.S.T. model as a guide to wording each goal. B.E.S.T. goals are believable, energizing, specific, and time bound.

Prioritize Your Goals

Once you have transferred all of the goals to the **6 Life Systems Pages**, stop and review each one. This single page encompasses your entire life plan in a particular category. And it is all on just one page!

Now, choose which goals are most important on each page. What demands your immediate attention?

Examine each category and decide which of them will be tackled within the next year. Try to pick at least one or two from each Life System so there is balance to your life. Ideally, you should have no more than 5-7 goals. Circle,star, or mark your choices on the page.

You may also want to break the long term goals into short-term segments. For example, if you wanted to earn a college degree this year you could apply, take an entrance exam, set aside funding, and target a date to begin your studies.

This method is simple, but it does require some extra work. In the end, you will have a detailed, hands-on map for the future. A little effort now will pay great dividends down the road. You will be able to reference your plan, tweak it, and check off each goal as it is met. If that sounds too overwhelming, simplify the process to fit your needs.

It's Never Too Late to Reach Your Goals!

Joyce was a WWII war bride. She came to the United States with love for her new husband and the hope of a better future.

But Joyce had a dream.

She wanted to earn a college diploma.

During the early years, Joyce was busy taking care of her family. It wasn't until later in life that she saw her dream become a reality.

In her late sixties, Joyce went back to college. After years of dedicated work, she graduated at the age of 74 with a Bachelor of Arts degree.

What would Joyce tell you? Don't give up on your dreams. It's never too late!

Chapter Nine

STEP #5: MAKE AN ACTION PLAN

When it is obvious that the goals cannot be reached, don't adjust the goals, adjust the action steps. Confucius

Lifetime and long-term goals provide direction to our life. The short-term and daily goals give us a plan of action. Our next step is put feet to our dreams and devise how we can accomplish them. We will develop an action plan. Our strategy is to work on a yearly schedule, but focus in 90 day increments.

Changing Our Habits

Setting goals means changing habits. And developing a new habit requires mental, physical, and emotional energy. It usually takes up to six weeks before one action becomes routine.

Research shows that every person has a certain threshold of energy that they may direct towards change. They can easily exhaust this energy by juggling too many goals. Then all of the effort and plans suffer.

We may enter into our action plan enthusiastically, but wear ourselves out in a few short weeks. Statistics show that 40% of people quit after six months. It is much better to start slowly.

Are you new to goal-setting? Start small. Be successful.

I recommend you begin with one or two goals. Focus your energies on them. Once achieved, add another target. As your confidence, desires, and skill set grow, you can add more. Soon you will be managing several at one time.

With that in mind, we can begin to develop a plan of action. Go at a slower pace if necessary, but make sure you are challenged. The following directions are for those who are ready to implement a multiple goal strategy.

The One Year Action Plan

The *One Year Action Plan* provides an overview of the upcoming year. It records all of your goals for the next 12 months and gives a general overview of your progress.

Transfer your chosen goal from the individual *Life System Pages* to the *One Year Action Plan.*

Record your yearly targets for each category in the appropriate places. Remember to begin with just one or two goals if you are just getting started.

The 90- Day Action Plan

The *90 Day Action Plan* is our primary focus and working document. It becomes our road map for the next three months.

We will direct our energy to several targets for this specific time frame. Then, at the end of this time period, we will reassess and develop the next *90 Day Action Plan.* During the course of a year, we will write four such plans.

Some of the goals in the first *90 Day Action Plan* will be carried over to the next. They require more time. Some goals may be accomplished in the first 90 days. Check them off the list.

For example...preparing for retirement. I might decide to start a 401k and sign up for my company's matching savings plan. Both of those actions are one-time events. Once they are done, I have met my goal! I can then add another goal to my list.

Each **Life System** is listed in the *90 Day Action Plan*. Underneath each category is a breakdown of steps to achieve the objective on a daily or regular basis. You will also find a reward box below each target. (Make a promise to yourself that as you reach each goal, you will celebrate!)

For our first 90 day window, we want to choose goals that are significant. Select those targets that will have the greatest impact. Ask yourself...

What three things can I focus on in the next 90 days that will produce the most significant impact?

These are your first targets.

Record them on the *90 Day Action Plan* sheet.

90 Day Action Plan

Spiritual Goals	Mental Goals	Professional Goals	Financial Goals	Social Goals	Physical Goals
Read the entire Bible in one year.			Make a budget and follow it	Invest daily time with my family	

Action Steps	Action Steps	Action Steps	Action Steps	Action Steps	Action Steps
Follow Bible reading plan			Make a list of expenses Read book by Dave Ramsey Create a budget Review spending habits weekly	Tell spouse and children "I love you" daily Schedulae a family fun night twice/month Go out to dinner with spouse monthly	

Reward	Reward	Reward	Reward	Reward	Reward
Purchase new study Bible			Plan a surprise getaway for family	Schedule a free day with friends	

www.pampelagri.com

Some of your targets require several contributing actions to achieve. Decide what activities you must do and record those.

In the example of losing weight, those actions might be:

- Drinking sixty-four ounces of water per day

- Exercising for thirty minutes, five days a week

- Eliminating sugar from your diet.

Record the actions under each goal.

These actions take priority. They become your "A list" of to-do items. You want to set aside the time and energy to ensure they are met on a daily/weekly basis. If you will give them the priority they deserve, you will obtain the results that you seek!

At the end of ninety days or the accomplishment of the goal, evaluate and focus for the next ninety days. Create a new *90 Day Action Plan* for the next three months.

Over the course of a year, we will have four 90 Day plans. We could choose up to 12 different goals, but some will be continued throughout the year. Be wise. Pace yourself and as you complete one, add another goal to your list.

Managing Multiple Goals

One way to include more goals in your routine is called "goal-stacking." In this method, combine several goals into one fluid action.

For example, if I wanted to exercise every day and read one leadership book every month, I could combine these. I might read on a treadmill or get the audio version of the book and listen as I ran. It's combining my time and linking one goal to another. Two or more can be completed in one block of time.

Goal stacking is efficient. It is an excellent way to maximize your time.

Chapter Ten

STEP #6: REVIEW YOUR GOALS

Review your goals twice every day in order to be focused on achieving them. Les Brown

As the 90 days unfold, review your goals on a daily basis. Constantly reading them does two things.

First, it activates the **RAS** brain function and stimulates our creative response. Second, it also reminds us of our targets and what we are working towards. We stay on course!

Once the *90 Day Action Plan* is complete, make copies and display them in highly visible places. I suggest placing both your *One Year Action Plan* and the *90 Day Action Plan* on a refrigerator door, bathroom mirror, or bulletin board.

You can review the goals in the morning as you brush your teeth, shave, or wash your face. You can also take a copy to work and read during the course of the day. Post it on your computer! Michael Hyatt makes screen savers for each of his goals.

As you read the plans, imagine how you will feel once you accomplish the target. Think about the positive effects on you, your family, and even your friends.

Revisit the rewards you promised yourself. Do they motivate you to keep going one more day?

Review your goals daily.

Keep them before your eyes.

> Make each day count by setting specific goals to succeed, then putting firth every effort to exceed your own expectations.
>
> Les Brown

Chapter Eleven

STEP #7: CELEBRATE

If you go to work on your goals, your goals will go to work on you. If you go to work on your plan, your plan will go to work on you. Whatever good things we build end up building us. Jim Rohn

As you hit your targets, celebrate! In fact, reward yourself as you accomplish each goal. It may be dining with your spouse at a favorite restaurant, reading a new best-seller, shopping for clothes in a smaller size, or planning a weekend getaway. Enjoy the process and reward yourself accordingly.

Setting and meeting goals takes time and effort. Don't skimp on this step. It will motivate you to continue and meet the next set of goals.

Final Words

Congratulations! Once you complete each of the *7 Easy Steps to Goal Setting Success*, you are now in control of your life. You have in your possession...

> • **A life outline with all of your hopes, dreams, and desires.**

> • **An understanding of the 6 Life Systems and how they fit into your plans.**

- **A yearly overview of your goals for the next 365 days.**

- **A 90 Day Action Plan to motivate and energize you to achieve your goals.**

- **A balanced and healthy approach to personal growth.**

You now have a road map for life.

As each 90 day period ends, re-evaluate. Look at your yearly targets, and plan accordingly for the next 90 days. Fill out a new *90 Day Action Plan* and continue with **Steps # 6 Review** and **#7 Celebrate**. I suggest you save a copy of these pages in a folder or binder for access at a later date.

But What If...

What happens if I slip and don't follow through with my action plan?

What if I overextend myself and I am struggling to meet my goals?

What if my goal isn't met in 90 days?

Should you panic? Get discouraged? Feel guilty?

No...don't give up!

Life happens. Some situations are out of our control. Pick yourself up, dust yourself off, and start all over again!

Part of the success in any endeavor is the process itself. What is working in you as you strive to achieve it?

Reset your goals and map out the next 90 days. Begin to move forward from where you are. Find a source of encouragement through a book, article, friend or family member.

Above all, look forward. Forget about what could have, would have, or should have been done. Start with a clean emotional slate by letting go of the guilt and frustration.

Goals are not meant to punish us, but to bring forth the potential that resides within. If it takes two years to write that book, then allow yourself the extra time. And don't feel guilty.

At the end of the current year, start the process all over again. This time you already have much of the work done. **Wrap Up** the old year. Review your **Goal-Storming Form** and add any new items. Assign new time frames. Prioritize once again. Develop your **One Year Action Plan** and a **90 Day Action Plan**.

Your life is waiting.

Set your goals.

Take action.

It's your life...live to the max!

If you enjoyed *7 Easy Steps to Goal Setting Success,* would you...

First, please go to *7 Easy Steps for Goal Setting Success* **at Amazon.com and leave a review about the book. I would appreciate your feedback.**

Second, tell your friends about the book. Invite some fellow goal setters to join you on your journey. Inspire and encourage each other along the way.

Finally, connect with me on my website and sign up for my newsletter. I would love to hear your story and how goal setting changed your life.

www.pampalagyi.com

Blessings!

About the Author

I am blessed to have a wonderful family. My husband Paul and I have traveled life's roads together. We enjoy working around the home, golfing, biking, travel, and a good movie...with lots of popcorn!

Since 1998, I have gone to five continents equipping and encouraging others through leadership development, personal growth seminars, mentoring, and conferences. I have served as a pastor, created and administered three Christian training centers, and mentored rising leaders from around the world.

I hold a Master of Divinity degree from Regent University. My publications include *Established: Seeking God's Plan for Spiritual Growth, Empowered: Igniting the Fire for Practical Ministry, The Word Became Flesh: Studies in the Gospel of John,* and *7 Easy Steps to Goal Setting Success.* I have plans for so many more!

God is the center of my life. He is my reason for living and it is his approval that I ultimately seek. I pray constantly that the words he gives me will bring life and wisdom to those who read and hear them.

Connect with Pam

Thank you for purchasing a copy of this book. For more information about my ongoing ministry, connect with me on my website at

www.pampalagyi.com

Sign up for my newsletter, download other resources, and become part of my blogging community. For more inspirational material, consider registering for my weekly blog on

www.theleadershipladder.com

And if you are a writer, check out my posts where I provide helpful tips on writing and the field of publishing at

www.theaspiringwriter.com

Other Books by Pam Palagyi

Available on Amazon!

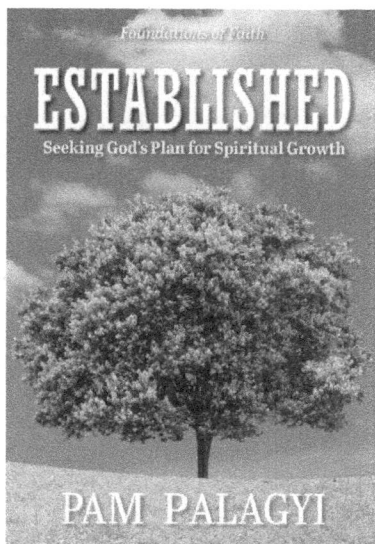

Are you experiencing all that God has to offer?

Have you asked yourself questions like...

Who am I and how do I relate to God?

Do I have a destiny, a God-directed plan for my life?

How can I overcome the daily obstacles and difficulties?

God created a perfect world. He planned for us to live a dynamic and fulfilled life within that realm. If your present lifestyle falls short of his best, then it is time to revisit the original design!

Established: Seeking God's Plan for Spiritual Growth unveils God's blueprint for success. When life began in the Garden of Eden, God provided five key elements essential to his plan. And you have a personal invitation to rediscover this garden!

www.ingramcontent.com/pod-product-compliance
Lightning Source LLC
Chambersburg PA
CBHW060611030426
42337CB00018B/3047